THE HOUSTON TEXANS

BY JOANNE MATTERN

EPIC

BELLWETHER MEDIA ★ MINNEAPOLIS, MN

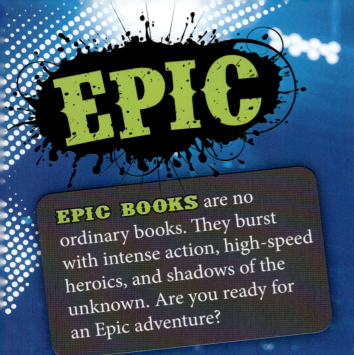

EPIC BOOKS are no ordinary books. They burst with intense action, high-speed heroics, and shadows of the unknown. Are you ready for an Epic adventure?

This book is intended for educational use. Organization and franchise logos are trademarks of the National Football League (NFL). This is not an official book of the NFL. It is not approved by or connected with the NFL.

This edition first published in 2024 by Bellwether Media, Inc.

No part of this publication may be reproduced in whole or in part without written permission of the publisher. For information regarding permission, write to Bellwether Media, Inc., Attention: Permissions Department, 6012 Blue Circle Drive, Minnetonka, MN 55343.

Library of Congress Cataloging-in-Publication Data

Names: Mattern, Joanne, 1963- author.
Title: The Houston Texans / by Joanne Mattern.
Description: Minneapolis, MN : Bellwether Media, 2024. | Series: Epic. NFL team profiles | Includes bibliographical references and index. | Audience: Ages 7-12 | Audience: Grades 2-3 | Summary: "Engaging images accompany information about the Houston Texans. The combination of high-interest subject matter and light text is intended for students in grades 2 through 7"-- Provided by publisher.
Identifiers: LCCN 2023021980 (print) | LCCN 2023021981 (ebook) | ISBN 9798886874785 (library binding) | ISBN 9798886876666 (ebook)
Subjects: LCSH: Houston Texans (Football team)--History--Juvenile literature.
Classification: LCC GV956.H69 M37 2024 (print) | LCC GV956.H69 (ebook) | DDC 796.332/64097641411--dc23/eng/20230518
LC record available at https://lccn.loc.gov/2023021980
LC ebook record available at https://lccn.loc.gov/2023021981

Text copyright © 2024 by Bellwether Media, Inc. EPIC and associated logos are trademarks and/or registered trademarks of Bellwether Media, Inc.

Editor: Betsy Rathburn   Designer: Jeffrey Kollock

Printed in the United States of America, North Mankato, MN.

TABLE OF CONTENTS

A PLAYOFF WIN!	4
THE HISTORY OF THE TEXANS	6
THE TEXANS TODAY	12
GAME DAY!	14
HOUSTON TEXANS FACTS	20
GLOSSARY	22
TO LEARN MORE	23
INDEX	24

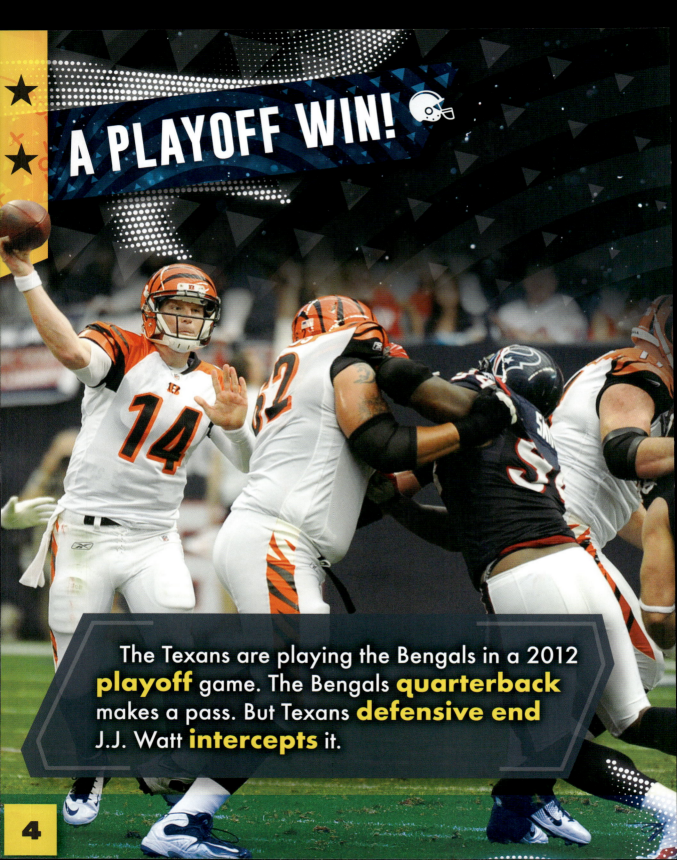

A PLAYOFF WIN!

The Texans are playing the Bengals in a 2012 **playoff** game. The Bengals **quarterback** makes a pass. But Texans **defensive end** J.J. Watt **intercepts** it.

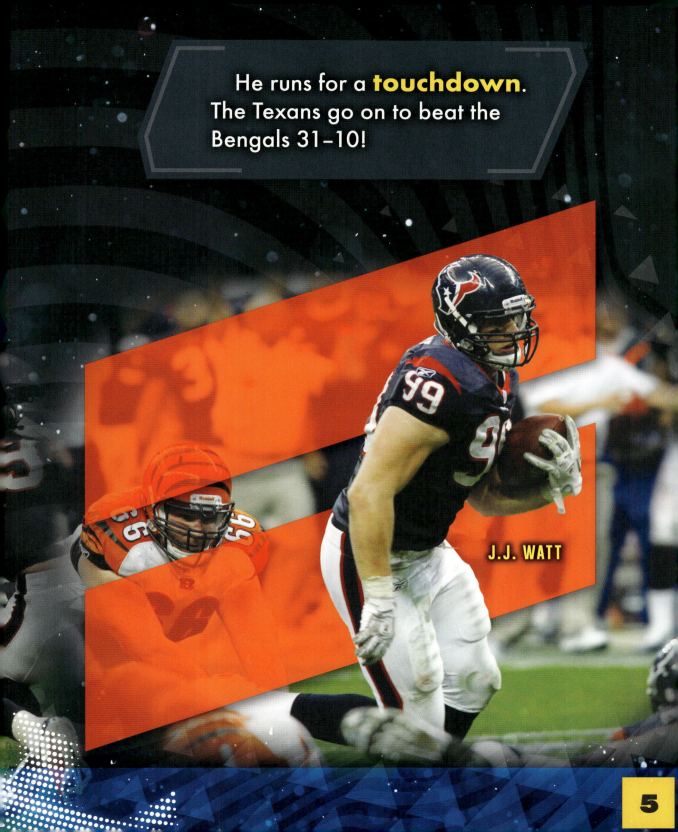

He runs for a **touchdown**. The Texans go on to beat the Bengals 31–10!

J.J. WATT

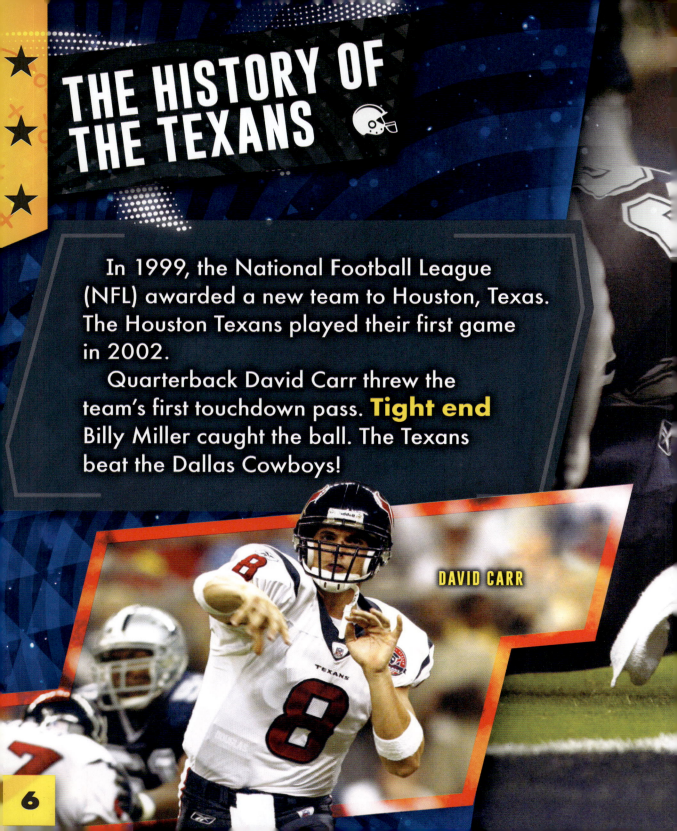

THE HISTORY OF THE TEXANS

In 1999, the National Football League (NFL) awarded a new team to Houston, Texas. The Houston Texans played their first game in 2002.

Quarterback David Carr threw the team's first touchdown pass. **Tight end** Billy Miller caught the ball. The Texans beat the Dallas Cowboys!

DAVID CARR

AT HOME IN HOUSTON

Houston was once home to the Oilers. In 1997, the team moved to Tennessee. Houston did not have a football team for several years.

BILLY MILLER

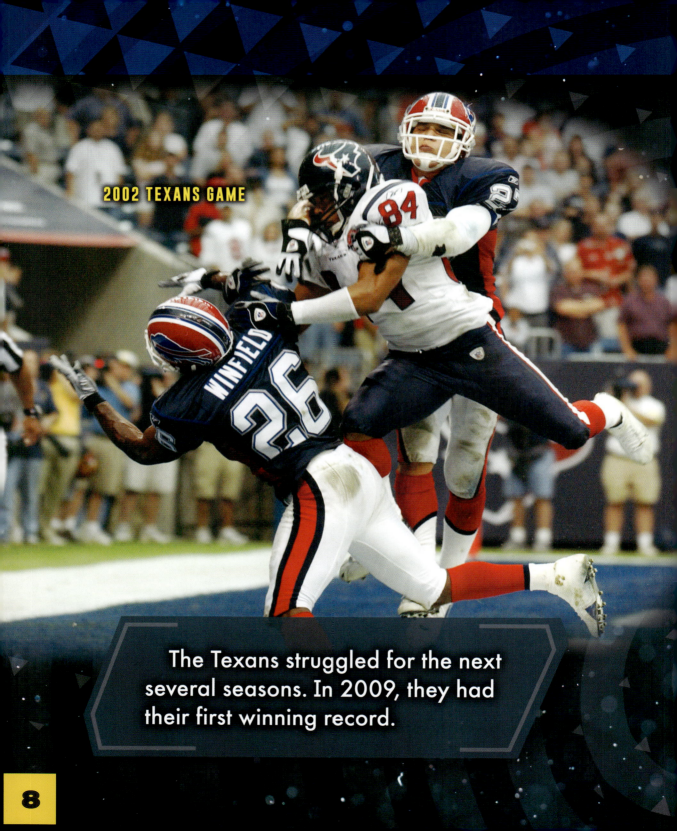

2002 TEXANS GAME

The Texans struggled for the next several seasons. In 2009, they had their first winning record.

NFL'S NEWEST

The Texans are the NFL's newest team!

In 2011, J.J. Watt joined the team. He helped them make the playoffs that season. They lost in the second round.

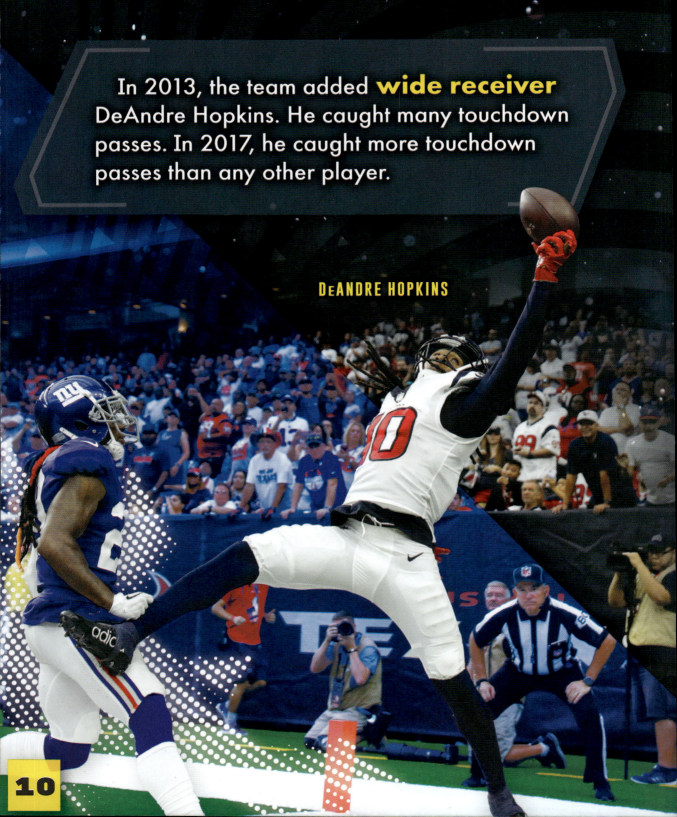

In 2013, the team added **wide receiver** DeAndre Hopkins. He caught many touchdown passes. In 2017, he caught more touchdown passes than any other player.

DeAndre Hopkins

The Texans made the playoffs a total of six times in the 2010s!

TROPHY CASE

PLAYOFF appearances
6

AFC SOUTH championships
6

THE TEXANS TODAY

TEXANS VS. TITANS

The Texans are part of the AFC South. They play at NRG **Stadium** in Houston, Texas.

12

Their top **rival** is the Tennessee Titans. The Texans hold the biggest win. They beat the Titans 57–14 in 2017!

📍 LOCATION 📍

NRG STADIUM
Houston, Texas

GAME DAY!

Fans wear red, white, and blue to Texans games. They wear their favorite players' jerseys.

They sing the team's fight song. They listen to the Deep Steel Thunder band at home games.

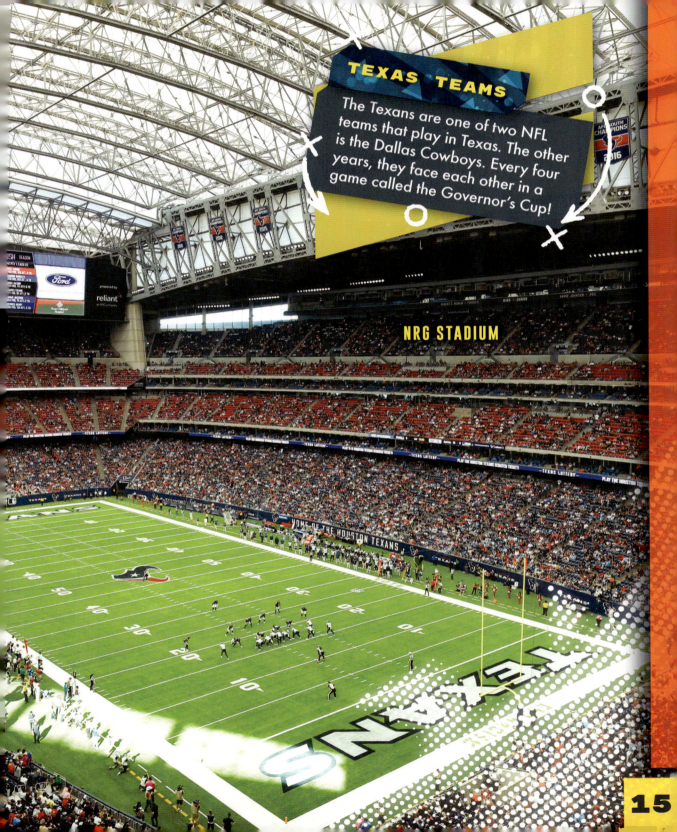

TEXAS TEAMS

The Texans are one of two NFL teams that play in Texas. The other is the Dallas Cowboys. Every four years, they face each other in a game called the Governor's Cup!

NRG STADIUM

Texans games start with a bang! Flamethrowers shoot fire. A cannon booms.

Toro, the team's bull **mascot**, runs onto the field. Fans cheer as the team races into the stadium.

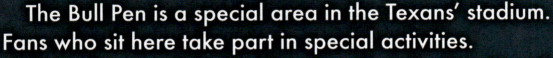

The Bull Pen is a special area in the Texans' stadium. Fans who sit here take part in special activities.

They cheer and stomp. They turn their backs when the other team scores. Texans fans are proud of their team!

★ FAMOUS PLAYERS ★

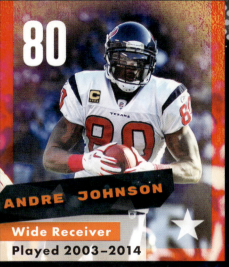

80
ANDRE JOHNSON
Wide Receiver
Played 2003–2014

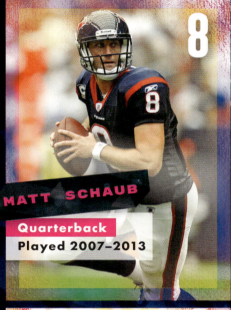

8
MATT SCHAUB
Quarterback
Played 2007–2013

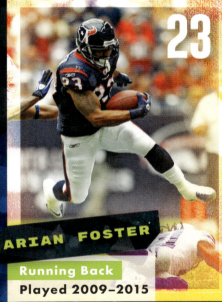

23
ARIAN FOSTER
Running Back
Played 2009–2015

99
J.J. WATT
Defensive End
Played 2011–2020

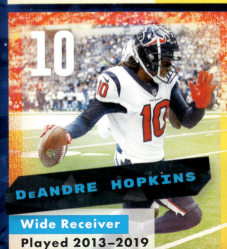

10
DeANDRE HOPKINS
Wide Receiver
Played 2013–2019

HOUSTON TEXANS FACTS

LOGO

JOINED THE NFL | 2002

NICKNAME | Bulls on Parade

MASCOT — TORO

CONFERENCE — American Football Conference (AFC)

COLORS

DIVISION | AFC South

 Indianapolis Colts

 Jacksonville Jaguars

 Tennessee Titans

STADIUM

★ **NRG STADIUM** ★
opened August 24, 2002

holds **72,220** people

20

🕐 TIMELINE

1999
The NFL awards a new football team to Houston

2002
The Texans beat the Cowboys in their first regular-season game

2011
The Texans make it to the playoffs for the first time

2019
The Texans reach the playoffs for the sixth time

2023
DeMeco Ryans becomes the team's head coach

★ RECORDS ★

All-Time Passing Leader
Matt Schaub
23,221 yards

All-Time Rushing Leader
Arian Foster
6,472 yards

All-Time Receiving Leader
Andre Johnson
13,597 yards

All-Time Scoring Leader
Kris Brown
767 points

21

GLOSSARY

defensive end—a player whose main job is to try to stop the opposing team's quarterback

intercepts—catches a pass thrown by the opposing team

mascot—an animal or symbol that represents a sports team

playoff—a game played after the regular season is over; a playoff game determines which teams play in the championship game.

quarterback—a player whose main job is to throw and hand off the ball

rival—a long-standing opponent

stadium—an arena where sports are played

tight end—a player whose main jobs are to catch the ball and block for teammates

touchdown—a score that occurs when a team crosses into their opponent's end zone with the football; a touchdown is worth six points.

wide receiver—a player whose main job is to catch passes from the quarterback

TO LEARN MORE

AT THE LIBRARY

Frederickson, Kevin. *DeAndre Hopkins.* Minnetonka, Minn.: Kaleidoscope Publishing, 2019.

Gigliotti, Jim. *J.J. Watt.* New York, N.Y.: Bearport Publishing, 2018.

Ryan, Todd. *Houston Texans.* Minneapolis, Minn.: Abdo Publishing, 2020.

ON THE WEB

FACTSURFER

Factsurfer.com gives you a safe, fun way to find more information.

1. Go to www.factsurfer.com.

2. Enter "Houston Texans" into the search box and click 🔍.

3. Select your book cover to see a list of related content.

INDEX

AFC South, 12, 20
Bull Pen, 18
Carr, David, 6
colors, 14, 20
Dallas Cowboys, 6, 15
Deep Steel Thunder, 14
famous players, 19
fans, 14, 17, 18
fight song, 14
Governor's Cup, 15
history, 4, 5, 6, 7, 8, 9, 10, 11
Hopkins, DeAndre, 10
Houston, Texas, 6, 7, 12, 13
Houston Oilers, 7

Houston Texans facts, 20–21
mascot, 17, 20
Miller, Billy, 6, 7
National Football League (NFL), 6, 9, 15, 20
NRG Stadium, 12, 13, 15, 17, 18, 20
playoffs, 4, 9, 11
positions, 4, 6, 10
records, 8, 10, 21
rival, 13
timeline, 21
trophy case, 11
Watt, J.J., 4, 5, 9

The images in this book are reproduced through the courtesy of: ASSOCIATED PRESS/ AP Images, cover (hero), pp. 1, 4, 9, 15, 21 (1999, 2019); digidreamgrafix, cover (stadium), p. 1; Justin Casterline/ Getty, p. 3; Unknown/ Alamy, pp. 5, 21 (2002, Matt Schaub, Arian Foster, Andre Johnson); Ronald Martinez/ Getty, pp. 6, 7; Harry How/ Getty, p. 8; Tim Warner/ Getty, p. 10; Bob Levey/ Getty, p. 12; Paparacy, p. 13; Cal Sport Media/ Alamy, p. 14, 19 (J.J. Watt); NFL/ Wikipedia, p. 15 (Houston Texans logo), 20 (Houston Texans logo, Indianapolis Colts logo, Jacksonville Jaguars logo, Tennessee Titans logo, AFC logo); Icon SportsWire/ Getty, pp. 16, 17 (inset), 18; Cooper Neill/ Getty, p. 17; UPI/ Alamy, p. 19 (Andre Johnson); Zuma Press Inc./ Alamy, pp. 19 (Matt Schaub, Arian Foster), 20 (mascot); Tribune Content Agency LLC/ Alamy, p. 19 (DeAndre Hopkins); Trong Nguyen, p. 20 (stadium); MCT/ Getty, p. 21 (2011); Bob Levey/ Getty, p. 21 (2023); Dilip Vishwanat/ Getty, p. 21 (Kris Brown); Kirby Lee/ Alamy, p. 23.